CW00661895

BOOKS ARE
COOL!
I LIKE CATS

LIFE ADVICE, INSPIRATION AND CATS

TOBY OLIVER DEAN

ISBN: 978-1-5272-5032-1

DO WHAT YOU WANT!

PUBLISHED BY I LIKE CATS PRESS, UK

ILIKECATSSHOP.COM

@TOBYILIKECATS

CONTENTS

Everyone wants to tell you what to do.
They tell you how to feel, how to act, what to wear, what to eat, what not to eat, how to be good, how to love, how to be healthy, how to be happy, how to live.

This book isn't that. This book is feeling good about yourself as you are. This book is telling you to ignore that other voice in your ear. This book is saying YES YOU CAN but if you don't want to YOU DON'T HAVE TO.

OK yeah, it's a bit of a contradiction but also tbh you can ignore everything in this book if you want, as long as you enjoy the cats.

YOU CAN DO THINGS

GOOD
THIN
TAKE

GS
TIME

BE

NICE

BUT
NOT
TOO
NICE

you
don't
have to
smile

DO

DO IT
TOMORROW

Do

YOU CAN FIND *friends* in UNLIKELY PLACES

MA
MIS

Do something that scares you

Mind y

ur business

Just because
you CAN
doesn't
mean you
SHOULD.

KEEP THE

NEGATIVITY

ON MUTE

9,876500 likes

notyrfriend oh my god I'm the best person in the world and I don't even try everyone else is a piece of trash #nofilter #humble #gross

OR BL

OCKED

OR

smash
your
phone
with
a
hammer

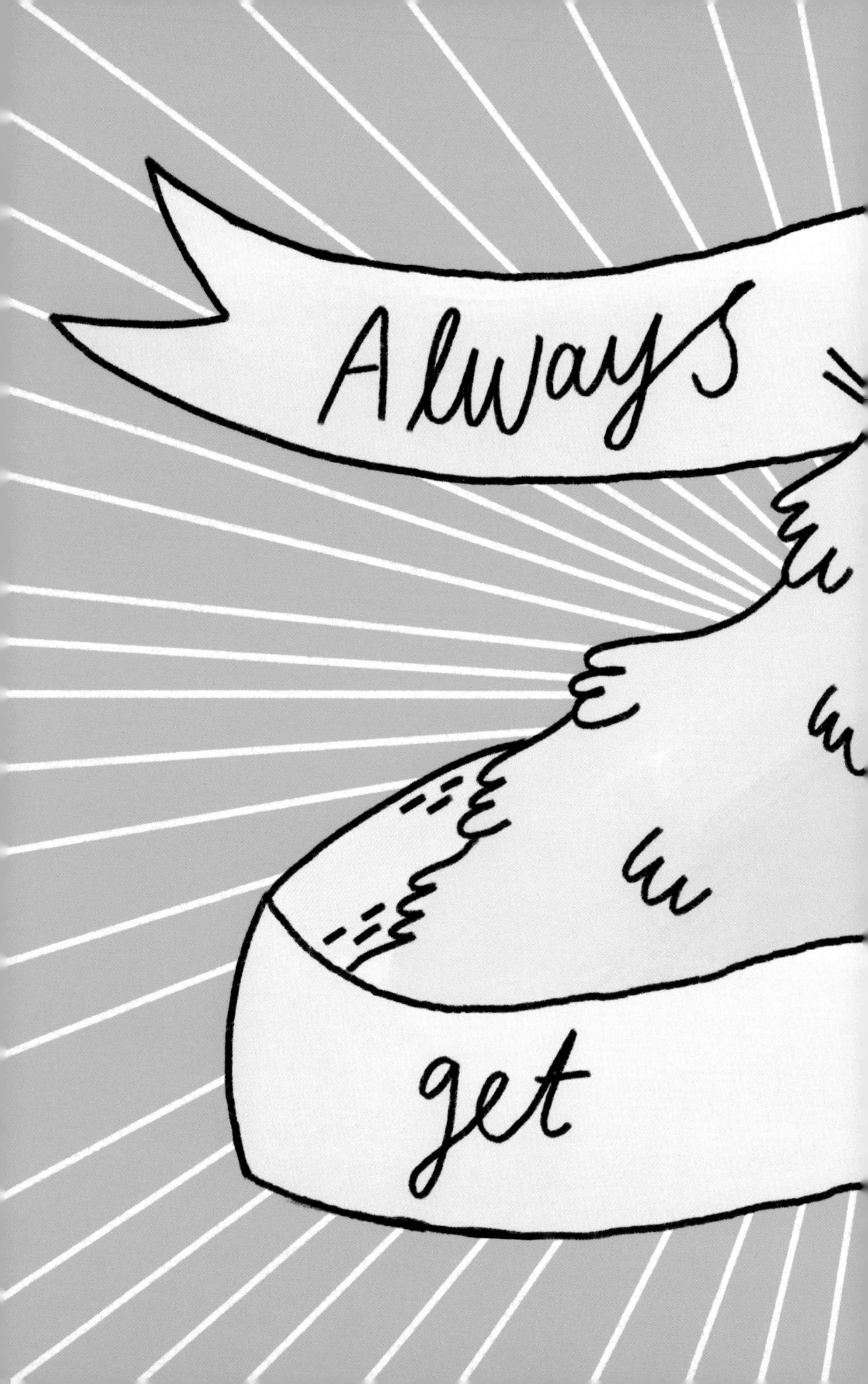
Always
get

$
£
Paid

IT'S OK TO
Bye
WHEN HORR

BE HAPPY
Now
LE PEOPLE DIE

CATS

BAD A

DVICE
WHICH IS STILL QUITE GOOD

if
DRE

u can

M IT

Stay asleep

MEOW CATS LP
WE WERE TWO COOL CATS ON THE RUN WE STOLE A CAR AND DIDN'T LOOK BACK.
DANGEROUS KITTY
I.L.C CATS
DANCE LIKE NOBODY'S WATCHING

EXCEPT YOUR
CAT IS ALWAYS
WATCHING
CATS
CATS
MEOW
Kitty

USE YOUR TEETH LIKE A WEAPON

BREAK
THE RULES

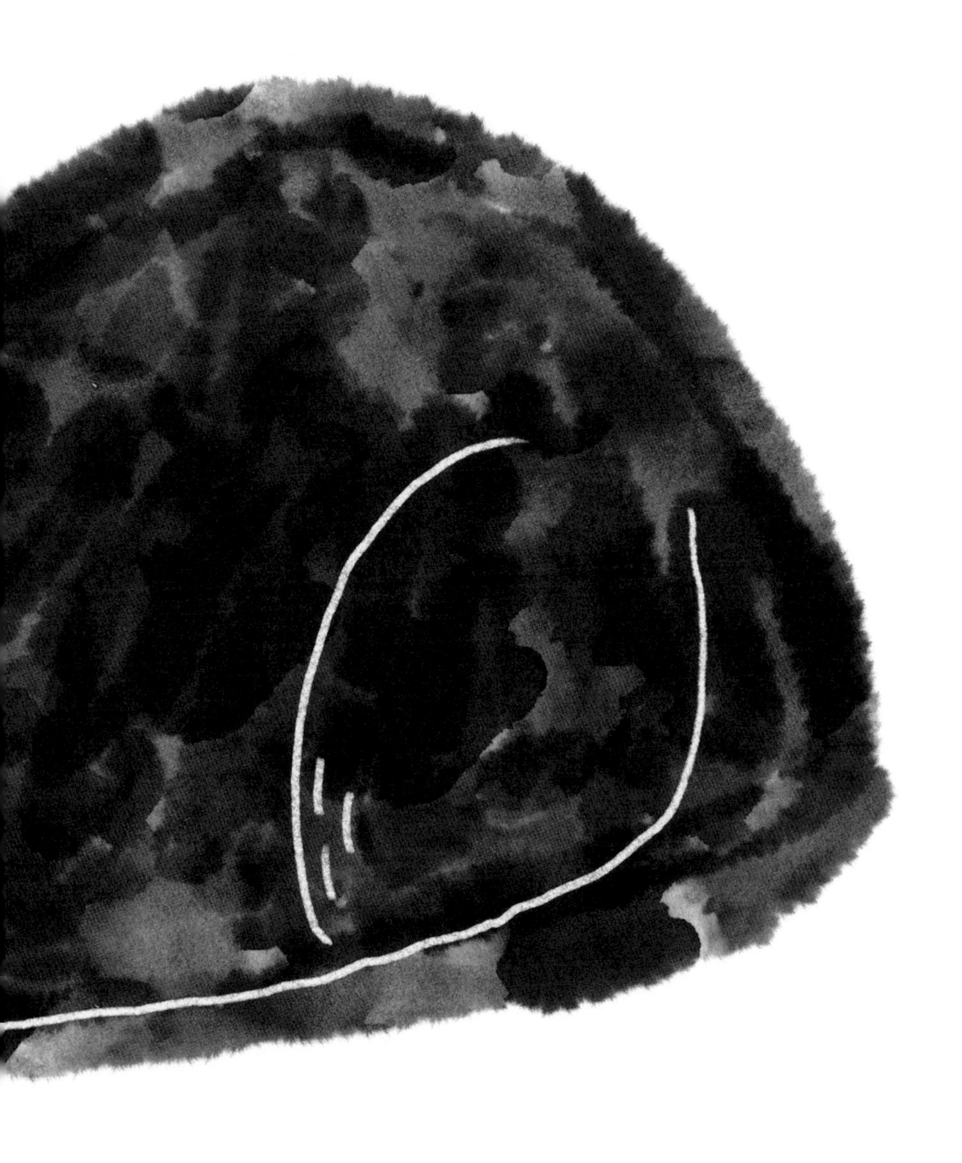

HELL yeah

Self
CARE

LIVE
LAUGH
LOVE
LUNCH

FRESH
CHOCAT
Kitty Cola
Golden Meows
Meow Break

MAKE SURE EV
WHEN IT'S YO

RYONE KNOWS
R BIRTHDAY!!!

STRET

C H

UNCLENCH
YO

JAW

EVERY BODY
IS A BODY

AND YOUR BODY BELONGS TO YOU

GIVE YOURSELF

SPACE TO GROW

Don't
Forget

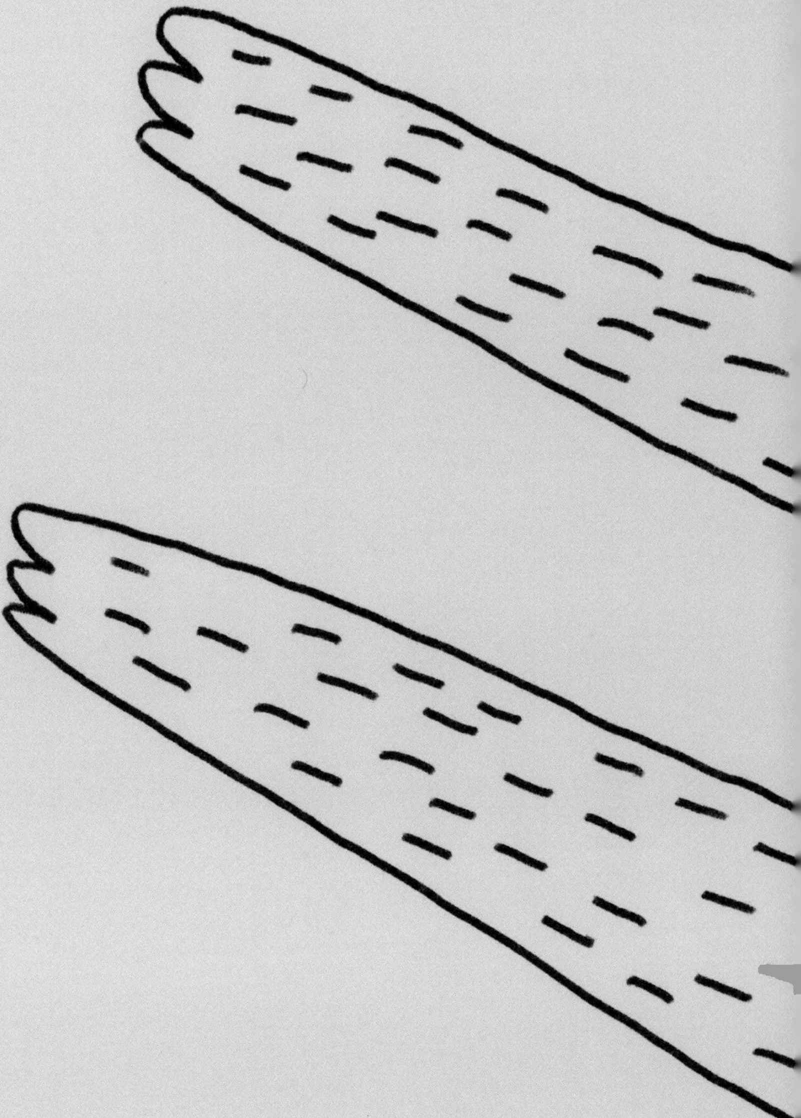

Water the plants

and water yourself

JUST BREATHE

IT

MIGHT

NOT

HAPPEN

THE
FUTU
DOES

RE
N'T
EXIST

BE

PEOPLE
ARE
JUST
PEOPLE

Nou
is p

ALL OF
YOUR ENEMIES
WILL DIE ☺

you'l

be

l

fine

you
are
not
alone

Cats are bet

r than people

DO WHAT YOU WANT